AUGSBURG

115 Farbbilder – colour photographs – photographies en couleur – foto a colori – fotos en color

Schmid Verlag Regensburg · Salzburg · Wien

Städtebildband 6

Augsburger Stadtchronik

15 v.Chr.: Es entsteht eine Siedlung durch Drusus, dem Stiefsohn des Kaisers Augustus. Er errichtet im Stammgebiet der keltischen Vindelicer ein Militärlager, das sich nach dem Abzug der Legionäre zu einer römischen Zivilsiedlung entwickelt.

1. Jh. n.Chr.: Als Augusta Vindelicorum bekannt, wird die Ansiedlung zur Hauptstadt der römischen Provinz Raetien.

3. Jh. n.Chr.: Einfälle der germanischen Alemannen zerstören die Siedlung.

832: Die Stadt wird erstmals unter dem Namen Augustburc geführt und ist Bischofssitz.

955: Entscheidende Abwehrschlacht gegen die Ungarnanstürme der Reiterscharen des Karchan Bult auf dem Lager Lechfeld. Unter Führung des Bischofs Ulrich an der Seite König Ottos I., des Großen, werden die Ungarn vernichtend geschlagen.

1276: Augsburg erhält das Stadtrecht zugesprochen und wird unter Rudolf von Habsburg freie Reichsstadt.

1431: Abschluß einer Jahrhunderte währenden Bauzeit am Dom mit der Weihe des Ostchors.

1432: Agnes Bernauer, eine Baderstochter aus Augsburg, wird Gemahlin von Bayernherzog Albrecht III.

1500: Die Stadt zählt ca. 20 000 Einwohner und ist Sitz der reichsten Kaufleute der Welt. Augsburg wird zum Mittelpunkt des deutschen Kunsthandwerks.

1518: Martin Luther verweigert den verlangten Widerruf seiner Thesen im Streitgespräch mit dem päpstlichen Legaten Cajetan.

1530: Reichstag im „goldenen Augsburg": Die protestantischen Fürsten überreichen die von Melanchthon verfaßte Bekenntnisschrift der lutherischen Kirche, die Augsburgische Konfession.

1555: Unterzeichnung des Augsburger Religionsfriedens zwischen Lutheranern und Katholiken. Dieser Beschluß hatte die Spaltung der Konfessionen in Deutschland zur Folge.

1624: Vollendung des Rathausbaues durch den Stadtbaumeister Elias Holl.

1648: Mit dem Westfälischen Frieden wird die Parität gesetzlich eingeführt. Dies bedeutet die Besetzung aller städtischen Ämter mit je einem Katholiken und einem Protestanten.

1710: Gründung der Reichsstädtischen Kunstakademie.

1805: Die Reichsfreiheit geht verloren und im folgenden Jahr wird Augsburg dem jungen Königreich Bayern angeschlossen.

1840: In der Stadt beginnt das industrielle Zeitalter. 12 000 Spindeln und 300 mechanische Webstühle sind im Betrieb, die Stadt wird an die Eisenbahn angeschlossen und Maschinenfabriken entstehen.

1897: Der erste betriebsfähige Motor, konstruiert von Rudolf Diesel, ist gebaut. Dies bedeutet neue Impulse für Industrie und Verkehrswesen.

1945: Durch die Bombardements der Alliierten wurden 4 600 Gebäude zerstört. Darunter etliche Baudenkmäler wie das Rathaus, der Perlachturm, der Fuggerpalast, das Weberhaus, zahlreiche Patrizierhäuser und 16 Kirchen.

1970: Eröffnung der Neuen Universität.

1972: Eröffnung des neuen Kongreßzentrums im Stadtpark.

1982: Das neue Zentralklinikum wird eröffnet.

1984: Sanierung des Rathauses und des Perlachturmes.

1985: Die Stadt feiert ihr 2 000jähriges Bestehen.

1988: Eröffnung des Messezentrums.

1996: Die historische Wiederherstellung des Goldenen Saales ist abgeschlossen.

1997: Grundsteinlegung für das Bayerische Landesamt für Umweltschutz. Anzahl der Studierenden an der Neuen Universität: 21 975.

A Short History of the City of Augsburg

15 B.C.: A settlement is founded by Drusus, stepson of the Emperor Augustus. In the area occupied by the Vindelicer, a Celtic tribe, he sets up a military camp, which develops into a Roman civilian settlement after the withdrawal of the legionaries.

1 A.D.: Under the name of Augusta Vindelicorum, the settlement becomes the capital of the Roman province of Rhaetia.

3 A.D.: The settlement is destroyed in raids by the Germanic Alemanni.

832 A.D.: First mention of the city by the name of Augustburc. It is now the seat of a bishop.

955 A.D.: A decisive defensive battle against the mounted Hungarian hordes led by Karchan Bult at the camp of Lechfeld. An Army under the combined leadership of Bishop Ulrich and King Otto I deals the Hungarians a devastating blow.

1276: Augsburg receives the status of a city and becomes a free imperial city under Rudolph of Habsburg.

1431: Long centuries of construction work on the cathedral are brought to a close with the consecration on the eastern choir.

1432: Agnes Bernauer, a barber's daughter from Augsburg, marries the Bavarian Duke Albrecht III.

1500: The city has about 20,000 inhabitants and the wealthiest merchants in the world reside here. Augsburg becomes the centre of German art.

1518: In the dispute with the papal legate Cajetan, Martin Luther is called upon to withdraw his theses, but refuses.

1530: The Imperial Diet takes place in 'Golden Augsburg'. The Protestant princes present the Lutheran Church with the confession of faith drawn up by Melanchthon, the Confession of Augsburg.

1555: The Religious Peace of Augsburg is signed by Lutherans and Catholics. This resolution led to the splitting of the confessions in Germany.

1624: The construction of the City Hall is completed by the master builder of the city, Elias Holl.

1648: As a result of the Peace of Westphalia, parity is introduced by law. This means that all municipal offices have to be occupied by both a Catholic and a Protestant.

1710: Foundation of the Academy of Art of the Imperial City.

1805: Augsburg loses its status as a free imperial city, and in the following year it is incorporated into the new Kingdom of Bavaria.

1840: The industrial age begins for the city. 12,000 spindles and 300 mechanical looms are in operation. The railway network reaches Augsburg and engineering works are set up.

1897: The first functional engine designed by Rudolf Diesel has been built. This means fresh impulses to industry and transport.

1945: 4,600 buildings were destroyed by the Allied bombings. Among them, several monuments such as the City Hall, Perlach Tower, Fugger Palace, 'Weberhaus', numerous patrician houses and 16 churches.

1970: Inauguration of the new university.

1972: Inauguration of the new Congress Centre in the City Park.

1982: The new Central Clinic is opened.

1984: Renovation of the City Hall and Perlach Tower.

1985: Celebrations are held in the city to mark its 2,000th anniversary.

1988: Inauguration of the Exhibition Centre.

1996: The historic restoration of the Golden Hall is completed.

1997: Laying of the foundation stone for the "Bavarian Office for the Preservation of the Environment." Number of students at the new university: 21,975.

Chronique de la ville d'Augsbourg

En l'an 15 avant J.-C.: Une cité est fondée par Drusus, beau-fils de l'empereur Auguste. Dans le territoire principal des Vindéliciens celtes il établit un camp militaire qui se transforme en cité civile romaine après le retrait des légionnaires.

1er siècle après J.-C.: Connue sous le nom d'Augusta Vindelicorum, la cité devient capitale de la province romaine de Rhétie.

3e siècle après J.-C.: La cité est détruite par des invasions des Alamans germaniques.

832: La ville est nommée Augustburc pour la première fois, elle est siège épiscopal.

955: Bataille défensive décisive contre les assauts hongrois des troupes de cavalerie de Karchan Bult sur le camp de Lechfeld. Sous la conduite de l'évêque Ulrich aux côtés du roi Otton 1er le Grand, les Hongrois subissent une défaite éclatante.

1276: Augsbourg obtient l'attribution du droit municipal et devient ville libre sous Rodolphe de Habsbourg.

1431: Après un siècle de construction la cathédrale est achevée par la consécration du chœur est.

1432: Agnès Bernauer, fille de barbier d'Augsbourg, devient l'épouse du duc de Bavière Albert III.

1500: La ville compte environ 20 000 habitants et est le siège des marchands les plus riches du monde. Augsbourg devient le centre de l'art allemand.

1518: Martin Luther refuse de révoquer ses thèses dans la controverse avec le légat Cajetan.

1530: Reichstag à «Augsbourg d'or». Les princes protestants présentent la Confession de l'église luthérienne rédigée par Mélanchthon, la Confession d'Augsbourg.

1555: Signature de la paix de religion d'Augsbourg entre luthériens et catholiques. Ce traité eut pour conséquence la division des confessions en Allemagne.

1624: La construction de l'hôtel de ville est terminée par le maître en bâtiment Elias Holl.

1648: Avec la paix westphalienne la parité est instaurée par la loi. Cela signifie que tous les postes municipaux sont occupés chacun par un catholique et un protestant.

1710: Fondation de l'école des beaux-arts de la ville impériale.

1805: Perte du statut de ville libre. L'année suivante Augsbourg est rattachée au jeune royaume de Bavière.

1840: Début du siècle industriel dans la ville. 12 000 fuseaux et 300 métiers à tisser mécaniques sont en service, la ville est reliée au chemin de fer et des usines de construction mécanique naissent.

1897: Rudolph Diesel construit le premier moteur en état de service. Ceci signifie de nouvelles impulsions pour l'industrie et le service des voies et communications.

1945: 4.600 bâtiments sont détruits par les bombardements des alliés. Parmi ceux-ci de nombreux monuments tels la mairie, la tour Perlach, le palais Fugger, la Maison Weber et des nombreuses maisons de patriciens ainsi que 16 églises.

1970: Ouverture de la nouvelle université.

1972: Inauguration du nouveau palais des congrès dans le parc municipal.

1982: Mise en service de la nouvelle clinique centrale.

1984: L'hôtel de ville et la tour Perlach sont rénovés.

1985: La ville fête sa deux millième année d'existence.

1988: Ouverture du centre des expositions.

1996: La reconstruction historique de la «salle d'or» est terminée.

1997: Pose de la première pierre de l'office fédéral bavarois pour la protection de l'environnement. Nombre des étudiants à la nouvelle université: 21 975.

Cronaca della città Augusta

15 a.C.: Druso, il figliastro dell'imperatore Augusto, fonda un centro abitato, un accampamento militare nella regione della stirpe celtica dei vindelici che, dopo il ritiro dei legionari, diventa un insediamento civile romano.

1° secolo d.C.: Noto come Augusta Vindelicorum, il centro diventa la capitale della provincia romana della Rezia.

3° secolo d.C.: Distruzione in seguito alle invasioni degli Alamanni germanici.

832: La città viene menzionata per la prima volta con il nome di Augustburc ed è sede espiscopale.

955: Battaglia decisiva di difesa dall'attacco della cavalleria ungherese guidata da Karchan Bult sul Lechfeld. Sotto la guida del vescovo Ulrico, leale all'imperatore Ottone I, sconfitta decisiva degli ungheresi.

1276: Augusta riceve i privilegi di una città e diventa città libera dell'impero sotto Rodolfo d'Asburgo.

1431: Fine della costruzione del duomo durata per secoli con la consacrazione del coro orientale.

1432: Agnese Bernauer, figlia di un barbiere di Augusta, diventa la sposa del duca di Baviera Albrecht III.

1500: La città annovera ca. 20.000 abitanti ed è la sede dei commercianti più ricchi del mondo. Augusta diventa il centro dell'artigianto artistico tedesco.

1518: Martin Lutero rifiuta di ritrattare le proprie posizioni nella disputa con il legato papale Caietano.

1530: Dieta dell'impero nell'"Augusta d'oro". I principi protestanti presentano la "Confessione di Augusta", la professione di fede della chiesa luterana redatta da Melantone.

1555: Stipulazione della "Pace di Augusta", fra luterani e cattolici. Questo documento ebbe come conseguenza la divisione delle confessioni in Germania.

1624: Termine della costruzione del palazzo del comune da parte di Elias Holl, "assessore all'edilizia" della città.

1648: Con la Pace di Vestfalia viene introdotta per legge la parità, cioè l'assegnazione delle cariche civiche rispettivamente ad un cattolico ed ad un protestante.

1710: Fondazione dell'Accademia d'Arte della città libera imperiale.

1805: Augusta perde il privilegio di città libera dell'impero e nell'anno seguente viene unita al regno di Baviera.

1840: Comincia l'industrializzazione: in città sono in uso 12.000 fusi e 300 telai meccanici, Augusta viene allacciata alla rete ferroviaria e nasce l'industria meccanica.

1897: Viene realizzato il prototipo di un motore su progetto di Rudolf Diesel. Ciò significa nuovi impulsi per l'industria ed i trasporti.

1945: I bombardamenti degli alleati distrussero 4.600 edifici, fra i quali numerosi monumenti come il palazzo del comune, la torre di Perlach, il palazzo dei Fugger, la Weberhaus, diverse case patrizie e 16 chiese.

1970: Fondazione della Nuova Università.

1972: Inaugurazione del nuovo Centro per congressi nel parco cittadino.

1982: Viene inaugurato il Zentralklinikum, la clinica universitaria.

1984: Ristrutturazione del palazzo del comune e della torre di Perlach.

1985: Ad Augusta, si celebrano i 2 000 anni della città.

1988: Inaugurazione del Centro fiera.

1996: Viene conclusa la fedele ricostruzione della "Sala aurea".

1997: Posa della prima pietra dell'Ente dello stato di Baviera per la tutela ambientale.

Crónica de la ciudad de Augsburgo

Año 15 a.d. J.C.: Druso, hijastro del Emperador Augusto, funda una colonia. Levanta un campamento militar en los dominios de la tribu celta de los vindelicios, que, tras la retirada de los legionarios, se convertiría en un asentamiento civil romano.

S. I d. J.C.: Dicho asentamiento, conocido con el nombre de «Augusta Vindelicorum», se convierte en la capital de la provincia romana Recia.

S. III d. J.C.: Las invasiones de los germanos alamanes destruyen la colonia.

832: Se designa, por primera vez, a la ciudad con el nombre de Augustburc. Es ya sede episcopal. Se levanta una iglesia sobre el sepulcro de la mártir Afra.

955: Decisiva batalla de defensa en el campamento Lechfeld contra los asaltos de las tropas húngaras de Karchan Bult. Los húngaros fueron exterminados bajo el mando del obispo Ulrico, aliado del rey Otón I el Grande.

1276: Augsburgo recibe el fuero urbano, convirtiéndose, bajo Rodolfo de Habsburgo, en ciudad imperial libre.

1431: Tras un siglo de duración, se concluyen los trabajos de construcción de la Catedral con la inauguración del coro oriental.

1432: Agnes Bernauer, hija de un cirujano de Augsburgo, se casa con el duque de Baviera Albrecht III.

1500: La ciudad cuenta con cerca de 20.000 habitantes, residiendo en ella los comerciantes más ricos del mundo. Augsburgo se convierte en centro del arte alemán.

1518: Martín Lutero se niega a retractarse de sus tesis en el debate con el legado pontificio Cayetano.

1530: Dieta de Augsburgo. Los príncipes protestantes presentan la confesión de fe de la iglesia luterana redactada por Melanchthon y conocida después como Confesión de Augsburgo.

1555: Firma de la Paz de Augsburgo entre luteranos y católicos. Esta decisión tendría como consecuencia la división de las Confesiones en Alemania.

1624: El arquiteco municipal Elías Holl termina la construcción del Ayuntamiento. Con ello se concluye la transformación de la ciudad medieval en una ciudad moderna.

1648: Con la Paz de Westfalia es introducida legalmente la igualdad de derechos. Esto significa que todos los puestos oficiales son ocupados por igual por católicos y protestantes.

1710: Fundación de la Academia del Arte de la Ciudad Imperial.

1805: Augsburgo pierde su estatuto de ciudad libre del imperio. Al año siguiente se integra en el joven reino de Baviera.

1840: Comienza en la ciudad la Era Industrial. 12.000 ruecas y 300 telares mecánicos entran en servicio, se establece la comunicación por ferrocarril y se crean fábricas de maquinaria.

1897: Se construye el primer motor ya listo para su puesta en servicio, diseñado por Rudolf Diesel. Un hecho que da nuevos impulsos a la industria y el transporte.

1945: Los bombardeos aliados destruyen 4.600 edificios. Entre ellos numerosos monumentos, como el ayuntamiento, la Torre de Perlach, el Palacio de los Fugger, «la Weberhaus» y otras casas patricias, además de 16 iglesias.

1970: Inauguración de la nueva Universidad.

1972: Inauguración del nuevo Centro de Congresos en el Parque Municipal.

1982: El nuevo Hospital Clínico Central abre sus puertas.

1984: Se sanean el Ayuntamiento y la Torre Perlach.

1985: La ciudad celebra sus 2.000 años.

1988: Se inaugura el Centro de Ferias.

1996: Se concluye la recuperación histórica de la Sala Dorada.

1997: Se coloca la primera piedra de la Delegación Provincial de Protección Medioambiental. El número de estudiantes matriculados en la nueva Universidad es de 21.975.

Augsburg von Osten, Stich mit Bezeichnungen der Baudenkmäler, 1746
Augsburg from the east, an engraving with the names of the architectural monuments, 1746
Augsbourg vu de l'est, gravure au burin avec descriptions des monuments, 1746
Vista di Augusta da est, incisione del 1746, con i nomi dei monumenti
Augsburgo vista desde el Este, grabado con descripción de los monumentos, 1746

Das Römermuseum in der barockisierten Dominikanerkirche St. Magdalena
Museum of Roman Remains in the Dominican Church of St. Magdalen, rebuilt in baroque
Le musée romain dans l'église dominicaine Ste Madeleine aux éléments baroques
Il museo romano nella chiesa domenicana di Santa Maddalena trasformata nel barocco
El Museo Romano en la barroquizada iglesia de los Dominicos de Sta. Magdalena

Vermutlich der vergoldete Kopf des Pferdes des Marc Aurel, Bestandteil eines Reiterdenkmals
Gilt horse's head, probably originally part of a statue depicting Marc Aurel on horseback
La tête dorée d'une statue équestre de Marc Aurèle vraisemblablement
La testa dorata del cavallo di una statua equestre dedicata probabilmente a Marco Aurelio
La cabeza dorada del caballo de una presunta estatua ecuestre de Marco Aurelio

Augustusbrunnen mit Allegorien der Augsburger Flüsse - Ausgrabungen aus der Römerzeit - Kaiser Augustus als Brunnenfigur, der Namensgeber der Stadt
The Augustus Fountain with allegories of the rivers of Augsburg - Roman excavations - Emperor Augustus, who gave his name to the city, as a figure above the fountain
La fontaine d'Auguste avec des allégories des fleuves arrosant Augsbourg - Fouilles de l'époque romaine - Statue de l'empereur Auguste auquel la ville doit son nom
Fontana di Augusto con allegorie sui fiumi di Augusta - Scavi romani - L'imperatore Augusto che ha dato il nome alla città, come statua di una fontana
La Fuente de Augusto con alegorías de los ríos augsburgueses - Excavaciones de la época romana - El Emperador Augusto, que dio nombre a la ciudad, coronando la fuente

Der im gotischen Baustil errichtete Dom, erbaut über einer 1065 geweihten romanischen Kirche

The Cathedral, built in Gothic Style over a Romanesque church consecrated in 1065

La cathédrale de style gothique, construite au-dessus d'une église romane consacrée en 1065

Il duomo costruito in stile gotico su una chiesa romanica consacrata nel 1065

La Catedral, de estilo gótico, construida sobre una iglesia románica, consagrada en 1065

Diese drei von insgesamt fünf Farbfensterdarstellungen aus dem Jahre 1140 in der südlichen Hochwand des Domes stellen die Propheten Oseas, David und Daniel dar
These three of the five portraits in the stained glass windows from the 4th decade of the 12th century show the prophets Hosea, David and Daniel
Trois des cinq vitraux des années 1140 du mur sud de la cathédrale, représentant les prophètes Osée, David et Daniel
Le tre vetrate policrome (sono cinque in tutto) appartengono alla parete alta meridionale del duomo (del 1140) e rappresentano i profeti Osea, Davide e Daniele
Los profetas Oseas, David y Daniel, tres de las cinco representaciones de la vidriera de los años 1140, en la pared sur de la Catedral

Gotischer Seitenaltar mit Fensterfront - ein Türgriff am Südportal - das um 1360 geschaffene Südportal des Domes mit Marienstatue am Mittelpfeiler
Gothic side altar with window front - a door handle of the south portal - The south portal of the Cathedral, sculpted in about 1360, with a statue of the Virgin Mary on the central column
Autel latéral gothique avec frontispice en vitrail - Une poignée du portail sud - Le portail sud de la cathédrale, datant de 1360, avec la statue de Marie sur le trumeau
Altare laterale gotico affiancato da vetrata - Una maniglia del portone meridionale - Il portale meridionale del duomo (1360) con statua di Maria sul pilastro centrale
Altar gótico lateral con vidriera - Una manilla de la puerta del Portal Sur - El Portal Sur de la Catedral (hacia 1360) con la estatua de la Virgen en el pilar central

Der Altar von Hans Daucher in der Fuggerkapelle von St. Anna
Altar by Hans Daucher in the Fugger Chapel of St. Anne's
L'autel de Hans Daucher dans la chapelle Fugger de Ste Anne
L'altare di Hans Daucher, nella cappella dei Fugger nella chiesa di Sant'Anna
El altar de Hans Daucher en la Capilla Fugger de Sta. Ana

Blick zum Gewölbe der Kapelle, 1512
Looking up to the vaulted ceiling of the chapel, 1512
Vue sur les voûtes de la chapelle, 1512
Guardando la volta della cappella, 1512
Vista de la bóveda de la capilla, 1512

Die Stadtpfarrkirche St. Ulrich und Afra, im Vordergrund die Ulrichskirche
The City Parish Church of St. Ulrich and St. Afra, in the foreground St. Ulrich's Church
Les églises paroissiales municipales St Ulrich et Ste Afra, au premier plan l'église St Ulrich
La parrocchiale di St. Ulrich und Afra, in primo piano la chiesa Ulrichskirche
La iglesia de San Ulrico y Santa Afra. En primer plano, la iglesia de San Ulrico

Die 1608 gebaute Orgel der Kirche St. Ulrich
St. Ulrich's Church: the organ, built in 1608
Les orgues de l'église St Ulrich construites en 1608
L'organo del 1608 della chiesa di St. Ulrich
El órgano de la iglesia de San Ulrico, construido en 1608

Blick auf die drei Choraltäre von Johann Degler aus den Jahren 1604 bis 1607
View of the three choir altars by Johann Degler dating from 1604 to 1607
Vue sur les trois maîtres-autel de Johann Degler, des années 1604-1607
I tre altari del coro di Johann Degler (1604-1607)
Los tres altares del coro de Johann Degler, construidos entre 1604 y 1607

Schmiedeeisernes Gitter von E.B. Bendel aus dem Jahre 1712
The wrought-iron lattice by E.B. Bendel, dating from 1712
Grille en fer forgé de E.B. Bendel, datant de 1712
Cancellata di ferro battuto di E.B. Bendel, 1712
Reja de hierro forjado de E.B. Bendel, del año 1712

Das aus dem 14. Jh. stammende Jakobertor mit seinem achteckigen Turmaufbau
St. James's Gate with its octagonal tower, dating from the 14th century
La porte Jacob datant du 14ᵉ siècle avec sa tour octogonale
La porta di S. Giacomo del trecento con la torre ottagonale
La Puerta de Santiago, del s. XIV, con su torre octogonal

Bildnis des hl. Christopherus am Jakobertor
St. Christopher, depicted on St. James's Gate
Portrait de St Christophe sur la porte Jacob
Ritratto di S. Cristoforo sulla porta di S. Giacomo
Imagen de San Cristóbal en la Puerta de Santiago

An der Stadtmauer: Frühbarocker Brunnen aus Venedig - der Steinerne Mann - der Fünfgratturm - eine Skulptur „die Hexe“

Along the city wall: early baroque fountain from Venice - the Man of Stone - The Pentagonal Tower - a sculptured figure, the “Witch”

Murailles de la ville: fontaine du début du baroque, de Venise - l'homme de pierre - la tour pentagonale - une sculpture «la sorcière»

Lungo le mura: fontana veneziana del primo Barocco - “Uomo di pietra” - la torre a cinque punte - una scultura detta “La strega”

En la muralla de la ciudad: Fuente barroca de Venecia - el Hombre de Piedra - la torre quíntuple - una escultura «la hechicera»

Teil des Jakoberwalls, eine um 1540 erbaute standhafte Stadtbefestigung
Part of St. James's rampart, a steadfast town fortification, built ca. 1540
Détail du «Jakoberwall», une fortification inébranlable de la ville, construite vers 1540
Scorcio del bastione di S. Giacomo, cinta muraria costruita verso il 1540
Los muros de Santiago, una sólida fortificación construida alrededor de 1540

Das Wertachbrucker Tor, ein achtseitiger Geschützturm, erbaut 1605
The Wertach Bridge Gate, an octagonal tower with artillery emplacements, built in 1605
La porte du pont Wertach, une tour d'artillerie octogonale construite en 1605
La porta del ponte sul Wertach, una torretta ottagonale del 1605
La Puerta del puente sobre el Wertach, una torre de defensa octogonal, de 1605

Blick in den Fronhof mit dem 1508 erbauten Residenzturm, früher bischöfliche Residenz
View of the Feudal Court and Residence Tower, built in 1508. Originally the bishop's residence
Vue sur la cour «Fronhof» avec la tour résidence construite en 1508, autrefois résidence épiscopale
Vista sul cortile Fronhof con la torre Residenzturm del 1508, già residenza vescovile
La antigua residencia episcopal con su torre residencial construida en 1508

Das Papsttor im Fronhof
The Pope's Gateway in the Feudal Court
La porte papale dans la cour «Fronhof»
La porta del Papa nel cortile Fronhof
La Puerta papal en la «Fronhof»

Der Höchstetter Erker am Senioratsbau der Fuggerei
The Hoechstett Oriel on the Signority Building of the Fuggerei
L'encorbellement Höchstett du bâtiment du conseil des anciens de la cité Fuggerei
Il bovindo di Höchstett nell'edificio del Consiglio degli anziani della Fuggerei
El torreón de Höchstett en el edificio del Consejo de Ancianos del barrio de Fuggerei

Die Augsburger Fuggerei, erbaut 1516-1523, ist die älteste Sozialsiedlung der Welt
Built between 1516 and 1523, the Fuggerei is the world's oldest welfare housing estate
La Fuggerei, la plus ancienne cité sociale du monde, construite de 1516 à 1523
La Fuggerei costruita fra il 1516 e il 1523, il primo quartiere d'assistenza sociale del mondo
La Fuggerei de Augsburgo, la colonia social más antigua del mundo (1516-1523)

Blick auf die St. Markuskirche und den Senioratsbau der Fuggerei
View of St. Mark's Church and the Signority Building of the Fuggerei
Vue sur l'église St Marc et le bâtiment du conseil des anciens de la cité Fuggerei
La chiesa di St. Markus e l'edificio del Consiglio degli anziani della Fuggerei
Vista de la Iglesia de San Marcos con el edificio del Consejo de Ancianos de la fundación de los Fugger

Der 70 m hohe Perlachturm aus dem 12. Jh. und das von Elias Holl zu Beginn des 17. Jh. errichtete Augsburger Rathaus, ein Symbol der Bürgermacht
The 230-foot Perlach Tower dating from 12th century and the City Hall, which was built by Elias Holl in the 17th century and testifies to the power of Augsburg's burghers
La tour Perlach de 70 mètres de hauteur, datant du 12e siècle, et l'hôtel de ville d'Augsbourg construit par Elias Holl au début du 17e siècle, symbole de la puissance bourgeoise
La "Torre di Perlach" alta 70 metri del XII secolo ed il palazzo del comune, simbolo del potere dei cittadini, costruito da Elias Holl all' inizio del XVII secolo
La Torre de Perlach, de 70 m de altura, data del s. XII y el Ayuntamiento de Augsburgo, construido por Elías Holl a comienzos del s. XVII, símbolo del poder burgués

Der nach Kriegszerstörung wiedererbaute „Goldene Saal“ im Rathaus mit geschnitzten Portalen, kassettierter Holzdecke und prunkvoller Wandmalerei
The City Hall's “Golden Hall”, rebuilt due to war damage, with carved portals, coffered wooden ceiling and magnificent mural painting
La «Salle d'or» dans la mairie, reconstruite après avoir été détruite pendant la guerre, avec ses portails sculptés, ses plafonds de bois à caissons et ses somptueuses peintures murales
La “Sala aurea” del Rathaus, ricostruita dopo le distruzioni della guerra, con portali intagliati, soffitto in legno a cassettoni e fastose pitture parietali
La «Sala Dorada» del ayuntamiento, reconstruida después de la guerra, dotada de portales tallados, techos artesonados y espléndidas pinturas murales

Die Fassade des Zeughauses, gestaltet von Joseph Heintz

The facade of the Armory created by Joseph Heintz

La façade de l'arsenal, de Joseph Heintz

La facciata dell'arsenale (Zeughaus), realizzata da Joseph Heintz

La fachada de la Armería, diseñada por Joseph Heintz

Die Bronzegruppe von Hans Reichle über dem Portal des Zeughauses
Group in bronze by Hans Reichle, over the portal of the Armory
Groupe en bronze de Hans Reichle au-dessus de la porte de l'arsenal
Il gruppo di bronzo di Hans Reichle, sopra il portone dell'arsenale
El grupo en bronce de Hans Reichle, sobre el portal de la Armería

Die Klosterkirche Maria Stern, die Johannes Holl in den Jahren 1574 bis 1576 erbaute
The Convent Church of Maria Stern, built by Johannes Holl between 1574 and 1576
La chapelle du couvent Maria Stern, édifiée par Johannes Holl dans les années 1574-1576
La chiesa del convento di Maria Stern costruita da Johannes Holl tra il 1574 ed il 1576
La iglesia conventual María Stern, construida por Johannes Holl entre 1574-1576

Der 1599 von Wolfgang Neidhard gegossene Merkurbrunnen
The Mercury Fountain, cast by Wolfgang Neidhard in 1599
La fontaine de Mercure, ouvrage en fonte de Wolfgang Neidhard datant de 1599
La fontana di Mercurio realizzata da Wolfgang Neidhard nel 1599
La Fuente de Mercurio, fundida por Wolfgang Neidhard en 1599

Augustusbrunnen vor dem Rathaus, die Figuren modellierte Hubert Gerhart
The Augustus Fountain in front of the City Hall, the figures moulded by Hubert Gerhart
La fontaine d'Auguste devant la mairie, les statues ont été modelées par Hubert Gerhart
La fontana di Augusto davanti al palazzo del comune, le statue sono di Hubert Gerhart
La Fuente de Augusto delante del ayuntamiento, las figuras fueron creadas por Hubert Gerhart

Augsburger Handwerkskunst - bemaltes Bürgerhaus in der Kapuzinergasse - kunstvoll gestalteter Türschmuck - die alte Silberschmiede mit blumengeschmücktem Erker

Augsburg craftsmanship: decorative paintings on a burgher's residence in Capuchin Lane - artistic ornamentation on a door - the Old Silversmith's with an oriel adorned with flowers

Artisanat d'Augsbourg - maison bourgeoise aux peintures décoratives dans la ruelle des Capucins - décor de porte artistique - l'ancienne orfèvrerie avec un encorbellement décoré de fleurs

Arte artigianale di Augusta - Palazzo cittadino dipinto nel vicolo Kapuzinergasse - Decorazione della porta artistica - La vecchia bottega d'argentiere con lo sporto infiorato

Arte artesanal de Augsburgo - Casa pintada en la Calle de los Capuchinos - Puerta artísticamente ornamentada - La antigua platería con mirador adornado de flores

Die Stadtmetzg, ehemaliges Schlachthaus, erbaut von Elias Holl 1609
The City Shambles, formerly the slaughterhouse, built by Elias Holl in 1609
Le «Stadtmetzg», ancien abattoir construit en 1609 par Elias Holl
Lo "Stadtmetzg", l´antico macello, eretto da Elias Holl nel 1609
El «Stadtmetzg», antiguo matadero público, construido por Elias Holl en 1609

Bürger- und Herrschaftshäuser der Stadt
Houses once owned by the bourgeoisie
Maisons bourgeoises de la ville
Palazzi cittadini e signorili di Augusta
Mansiones burguesas y señoriales de la ciudad

Blick vom Milchberg auf die Spitalkirche St. Margareth und den Wollmarkt
View of the Milchberg with the church of St. Margaret's Hospice and the Wollmarkt
Vue sur la Milchberg avec l'église de l'hôpital Ste Marguerite et le marché à laine
Vista dal Milchberg sulla chiesa di St. Margareth e sul Wollmarkt (mercato della lana)
El Milchberg con la iglesia del hospital Sta. Margarita y el mercado de lanas

Die beiden sechseckigen Wassertürme, die vom 15. bis 17. Jahrhundert erbaut wurden, im Hintergrund das Rote Tor
The two hexagonal water towers, built in the 15th to 17th centuries with the Red Gate in the background
Les deux tours d'eau hexagonales qui ont été construites du 15ᵉ au 17ᵉ siècle, la porte Rouge à l'arrière-plan
Le due torri esagonali dell'acqua, costruite tra il XV ed il XVII secolo, sullo sfondo la Porta rossa
Las dos torres exagonales del agua, construidas en los siglos XV al XVII; al fondo, la Puerta Roja

Das Schaezlerpalais in der Maximilianstraße, erbaut von Liebert von Liebenhofen, 1770
The Schaezler Palace in Maximilian Street, built by Liebert von Liebenhofen in 1770
Le palais Schaezler rue Maximilian, construit par Liebert von Liebenhofen, 1770
Il Palazzo Schaezler nella via Maximilianstrasse, costruito da L. von Liebenhofen, nel 1770
El Palacio Schaezler en la Calle Maximiliano, construido por L. von Liebenhofen en 1770

Der vor dem Palais stehende, 1602 vollendete Herkulesbrunnen
In front of the Palace stands the Hercules Fountain, completed in 1602
La fontaine d'Hercule devant le palais, achevée en 1602
La Fontana di Ercole del 1602, davanti al palazzo
Delante del Palacio, la Fuente de Hércules, terminada en 1602

Blick in den prächtigen Festsaal des Schaezlerpalais, für den Gregorio Guglielmi 1767 das Deckengemälde schuf
The impressive stately hall of the Schaezler Palace. The ceiling was created by Gregorio Guglielmi in 1767
Vue dans la somptueuse salle d'apparat du palais Schaezler, dont Gregorio Guglielmi fit la fresque de plafond en 1767
Scorci della magnifica sala delle feste del palazzo Schaezler, per la quale Gregorio Guglielmi nel 1767 eseguì il dipinto del soffitto
El fastuoso salón de fiestas del Palacio Schaezler, para el que Gregorio Guglielmi pintó en 1767 el fresco del techo

Das 1855 gegründete Maximilianmuseum führt durch die Stadtgeschichte und das Kunstgewerbe von Alt-Augsburg
In the Maximilian-Museum, founded in 1855, one can retrace the history of the city and its art and crafts
Le musée Maximilian, fondé en 1855, conduit à travers l'histoire de la ville et les arts appliqués du vieil Augsbourg
Il Museo Massimiliano fondato nel 1855 rappresenta la storia urbana e l'artigianato della vecchia Augusta
El Museo Maximiliano, fundado en 1855, nos muestra la historia de la ciudad y las artes y oficios del viejo Augsburgo

Städtische Kunstsammlung: Funeralhelm Kaiser Karls V. von Anton Pfeffenhausen
The Municipal Art Collection: Emperor Charles V's funeral helmet, by A. Pfeffenhausen
Galerie d'art municipale: Casque funéraire de l'empereur Charles V d'A. Pfeffenhausen
Collezione d'Arte Comunale: elmo funerario dell'imperatore Carlo V di Anton Pfeffenhausen
Museo municipal: Casco funerario del Emperador Carlos V, de Anton Pfeffenhausen

Städtische Kunstsammlung: Ewiger Kalender, kunstvolle Arbeit v. J.A.Thelott, ca. 1690
The Municipal Art Collection: an eternal calendar, craftsmanship by J.A.Thelott, ca. 1690
Galerie d'art municipale: Calendrier perpétuel, œuvre d'art de J.A.Thelott, vers 1690
Collezione d'Arte Comunale: Calendario perpetuo, lavoro artistico di J.A.Thelott (ca. 1690)
Museo municipal: Calendario perpetuo, trabajo artístico de J.A.Thelott, hacia 1690

Staatsgalerie Augsburg: Szene aus dem Leben des Apostel Paulus von Hans Holbein dem Älteren
The State Gallery, Augsburg: Scene from the Life of the Apostle Paul, by Hans Holbein the Elder
Galerie nationale d'Augsbourg: Scène de la vie de l'apôtre Paul, de Hans Holbein l'Ancien
Galleria di Stato di Augusta: La "scena dalla vita dell'apostolo Paolo" di Hans Holbein il Vecchio
Galería Nacional: escenas de la vida del Apóstol Pablo, de Hans Holbein el Viejo

Staatsgalerie Augsburg: Bildnis Jakob Fuggers des Reichen (1459-1525) von Albrecht Dürer

The State Gallery, Augsburg: Portrait of Jakob Fugger the Rich (1459-1525), by Albrecht Dürer

Galerie nationale d'Augsbourg: Portrait de Jacob Fugger le riche (1459-1525), d'Albrecht Dürer

Galleria di Stato di Augusta: Ritratto di Jacob Fugger detto il Ricco (1459-1525) di Albrecht Dürer

Galería Nacional: retrato de Jakob Fugger el Rico (1459-1525), de Alberto Durero

Städtische Kunstsammlung: Opfer an Diana von Johann Heinrich Schönfeld, um 1640
The Municipal Art Collection: A Sacrifice for Diana, by Johann Heinrich Schönfeld, ca. 1640
Galerie d'art municipale: Offrande à Diane de Johann Heinrich Schönfeld, 1640 environ
Collezione d'Arte Comunale: Immolazione a Diana di Johann Heinrich Schönfeld (verso il 1640)
Museo municipal: Sacrificio a Diana, de Johann Heinrich Schönfeld, hacia 1640

Städtische Kunstsammlung im Schaezler-palais: Bildnis einer Unbekannten von Johann Heinrich Tischbein, um 1753

The Municipal Art Collection in the Schaezler Palace: Portrait of an Unknown Woman, by Johann Heinrich Tischbein, ca. 1753

Galerie d'art municipale dans le palais Schaezler: Portrait d'une inconnue de Johann Heinrich Tischbein, 1753 environ

Collezione d'Arte Comunale nel "Palazzo Schaezler": Ritratto di donna ignota di Johann Heinrich Tischbein (verso il 1753)

Museo municipal en el Palacio Schaezler: Retrato de una desconocida, de Johann Heinrich Tischbein, hacia 1753

„Die Begegnung“, 1985, im Wolfgang-Lettl-Atrium, Museum für surreale Kunst
"The Encounter" ('Die Begegnung'), 1985, in the Wolfgang Lettl atrium, Museum of Surreal Art
«La rencontre», 1985, dans l' «Atrium Wolfgang Lettl», Musée de l'art surréaliste
"L´incontro", 1985, nel Wolfgang-Lettl-Atrium, Museo di arte surreale
«Die Begegnung» (El Encuentro), 1985, en el Atrio de Wolfgang-Lettl del Museo de Arte Surreal

MAN-Museum: die ersten MAN-Fahrzeug-Dieselmotoren - der erste Versuchsmotor von Rudolf Diesel - ein Einzylindermotor von 1905 - eine Druckerei Schnellpresse aus dem Jahre 1912
The MAN Museum: the first MAN diesel engines for motor vehicles - the first experimental engine by Rudolf Diesel - a one-cylinder engine (1905) - a flatbed printing machine (1912)
Le musée MAN: les premiers moteurs Diesel MAN - le premier moteur d'essai de Rudolph Diesel - un moteur à un cylindre de 1905 - une presse mécanique d'imprimerie de 1912
Museo MAN: i primi motori diesel della MAN - il primo motore sperimentale di Rudolf Diesel - un motore a un cilindro del 1905 - una macchina da stampa veloce per tipografia del 1912
El Museo de MAN: los primeros vehículos de MAN con motor diesel - el primer motor de ensayo de Rudolf Diesel - motor de un cilindro de 1905 - una prensa rápida de imprenta de 1912

Die Universität Augsburg, eröffnet 1970
The University of Augsburg, inaugurated in 1970
L'université d'Augsbourg, inaugurée en 1970
L'università di Augusta aperta nel 1970
La Universidad de Augsburgo, inaugurada en 1970

Eingangshalle zum Augsburger Messegelände
Entrance hall to the Augsburg fairground
Hall d'entrée du terrain de la foire d'Augsbourg
L'entrata al Centro fiera di Augusta
La entrada de la Feria de Augsburgo

Das 1972 eröffnete Kongreßzentrum bietet Platz für Tagungen, gesellschaftliche Veranstaltungen, Konzerte und Theateraufführungen
The Congress Centre, opened in 1972, offers facilities for conferences, social functions, concerts and dramatic productions
Le palais des congrès inauguré en 1972, centre de congrès, spectacles mondains, concerts et représentations théâtrales
Il centro per congressi aperto nel 1972 che offre spazio per congressi, serate in società, concerti e rappresentazioni di teatro
El Centro de Congresos, inaugurado en 1972; en él se celebran congresos, recepciones, conciertos y representaciones teatrales

Das Foyer im Zentrum der Kongreßhalle
The foyer in the centre of the Congress Hall
Le foyer au centre du hall des congrès
La hall al centro del salone dei congressi
La sala vestíbulo del Centro de Congresos

Straßenschauspieler ziehen zum Theaterfest
Street actors on their way to the drama festival
Acteurs ambulants se rendant à la fête théâtrale
Attori ambulanti che vanno alla festa del teatro
Actores ambulantes camino de una fiesta teatral

Das 1867 erbaute und 1956 nach Kriegszerstörung wiedereröffnete Stadttheater, im Hintergrund die Hl. Kreuzkirche
The Municipal Theatre, built in 1867, suffered considerable war damage, but was re-opened in 1956, the Church of the Holy Cross in the background
Le théâtre municipal construit en 1867 et réouvert en 1956 après sa destruction pendant la guerre, à l'arrière-plan l'église de la Sainte Croix
Il Teatro Municipale costruito nel 1867 e riaperto nel 1956, dopo la distruzione durante la guerra
El Teatro municipal, construido en 1867, fue destruido en la guerra, abriéndose de nuevo en 1956, al fondo la Iglesia de la Santa Cruz

Leopold Mozart, der Vater von Wolfgang Amadeus, wurde in Augsburg 1719 geboren
Leopold Mozart, Wolfgang Amadeus's father, was born in Augsburg in 1719
Léopold Mozart, père de Wolfgang Amadeus, né à Augsbourg en 1719
Leopold Mozart, il padre de Wolfgang Amadeus, nacque qui, nel 1719
Leopold Mozart, el padre de Wolfgang Amadeus, nació en Augsburgo en 1719

Das Mozarthaus in der Frauentorstraße, heute das Mozartmuseum
The Mozart House in Lady Gate Street, today the Mozart Museum
Le musée de Mozart dans la maison de Mozart, Frauentorstrasse
La casa di Mozart nella Frauentorstrasse che oggi ospita il Museo di Mozart
La Casa de Mozart en la Calle Frauentor, hoy Museo de Mozart

Geburtshaus des Dichters Bertolt Brecht, jetzt das „Brechthaus“ mit neugestalteten Ausstellungsräumen über seine Werke
Birthplace of the poet Bertolt Brecht, now the “Brecht House” with refurbished exhibition rooms about his works
Maison natale du poète Bertolt Brecht, à présent «Maison de Brecht» avec les salles d’exposition sur son œuvre, nouvellement aménagées
La casa natale dello scrittore Bertold Brecht, ora “Brechthaus”, con nuove sale di esposizione sulla sua attività letteraria
Casa natal del escritor Bertolt Brecht, ahora renovada como la «Casa de Brecht», en cuyas salas se exponen los trabajos del artista

Das Rote Tor wurde 1622 von Elias Holl als Wachturm an der Stadtmauer errichtet
The Red Gate was erected by Elias Holl in 1622 as a watchtower on the city wall
La porte Rouge fut contruite en 1622 par Elias Holl, comme tour de guet des fortifications de la ville
La Porta rossa venne costruita nel 1622 da Elias Holl come torre di guardia delle mura cittadine
La Puerta Roja, construida en 1622 por Elías Holl como torre de vigía en las murallas de la ciudad

Opernaufführung auf der Freilichtbühne am Roten Tor
An opera being performed on the open-air stage at the Red Gate
Opéra au théâtre en plein air près de la tour Rouge
Rappresentazione d'opera nel teatro all'aperto presso la "Porta Rossa"
Representación de una ópera al aire libre junto a la Puerta Roja

„Bill Bo und seine Bande", Figuren der weltbekannten Augsburger Puppenkiste
"Bill Bo and his Band", marionettes from the world-famous Augsburg Puppet Show
«Bild Bo et sa bande», personnages du théâtre de marionnettes de renommée mondiale
"Bill Bo e la sua banda", personaggi del famoso teatro di marionette di Augusta
«Bill Bo y su banda», figuras del mundialmente famoso guiñol de Augsburgo

Die St. Annakirche inmitten der Fußgängerzone mit Goldschmiedekapelle, Familiengrabstätte der Fugger und übereckgestellten Turm von Elias Holl
The Church of St. Anne in the middle of the pedestrian area with Goldsmith's Chapel, Fugger family tombs and, at the corner, Elias Holl's tower
L'église Ste Anna au centre de la zone piétonnière, avec sa chapelle d'orfèvre, ses tombeaux de la famille Fugger et sa tour en travers d'Elias Holl
Nella zona pedonale la chiesa di St. Anna con la Cappella degli orafi, sepolcro di famiglia dei Fugger e torre di Elias Holl
La Iglesia de Santa Ana en la zona peatonal, con la Capilla de los Orfebres, panteón de los Fugger. En la esquina, una torre de Elías Holl

Einkauf in der Annastraße, Teil der Fußgängerzone
Shopping in St. Anne's Street, part of the pedestrian area
Courses rue Anna, partie de la zone piétonne
Shopping nella Annastrasse, parte della zona pedonale
De compras por la Plaza Moritz y la Annastrasse en la zona peatonal

Gastronomie in der historischen „Welser Kuchl“ und gastliche Bewirtung vor dem Rathaus
Culinary delights in the historical "Welser Kitchen", relaxing in front of the City Hall
Gastronomie dans le restaurant historique «Kuchl» de Welser, et café devant l'hôtel de ville
Specialità tradizionali nella trattoria „Welser Kuchl“ e pausa all´aperto davanti al palazzo del comune
Gastronomía en la histórica «Welser Kuchl» y horas placenteras delante del ayuntamiento

Bilder vom beliebten Stadtmarkt im Herzen der Fußgängerzone

Pictures of the popular City Market in the heart of the pedestrian precinct

Images du marché de la ville au cœur de la zone piétonne

Immagini del mercato cittadino nel cuore della zona pedonale

Escenas del popular mercado de la ciudad en el corazón de la zona peatonal

Mit dem Augsburger Bürgerfest wird in historischen Kostümen und farbenprächtigen Umzügen die Vergangenheit der Stadt wieder lebendig
With the Augsburg city festival, the history of the town comes back to life in historic costumes and colourful processions
Grâce à la fête des citoyens d'Augsbourg, le passé de la ville revit dans ses costumes historiques et ses défilés riches en couleurs
Durante la festa della città il passato rivive nei costumi storici e nelle coloratissime sfilate
Las fiestas de Augsburgo se celebran con trajes de época y desfiles llenos de colorido, durante los que se revive el pasado de la ciudad

Eine idyllische Fahrt mit dem Ruderboot am Oblatterwall, einem Teil des ehemaligen Stadtgrabens
An idyllic trip in a rowing boat along the "Oblatterwall" part of the former moat around the city
Promenade idyllique en bateau à rames sur le «Oblatterwall», partie de l'ancien fossé de la ville
Una gita in barca a remi idilliaca lungo il bastione Oblatter, una parte dell'antico fossato attorno alla città
Paseo idílico en barca por el «Oblatterwall», una parte de los antiguos fosos de la ciudad

Ein Spaß für Jung und Alt: Das Augsburger Volksfest, der Oster- und Herbstplärrer
Fun for young and old: Augsburg's Easter and autumn fair, the "Plärrer"
Plaisir pour jeunes et vieux: les fêtes populaires d'Augsbourg de Pâques et d'automne, appelées «Plärrer»
Un divertimento per giovani ed anziani: La festa popolare di Augusta detta Plärrer, organizzata prima di Pasqua ed in autunno
Diversión para pequeños y mayores: la Feria de Augsburgo, llamada «Plärrer» se celebra en Pascua y en otoño

Ballonfahren, eine alte Augsburger Tradition
Travelling by balloon, an old Augsburg tradition
Sport aérostatique, une vieille tradition des Augsbourgeois
Viaggi in areostato, un'antica tradizione di Augusta
Los vuelos en globo, una antigua tradición en Augsburgo

Das Rosenaustadion mit einem Fassungsvermögen von über 40 000 Besuchern
The Rosenau Stadium with a capacity of over 40,000 spectators
Le stade Rosenau pouvant accueillir 40 000 spectateurs
Lo stadio Rosenau con una capienza di oltre 40.000 spettatori
El estadio de Rosenau da cabida a más de 40.000 espectadores

Zu den Olympischen Spielen 1972 erbaut, das erste Kanu-Slalom-Stadion der Welt am Augsburger Eiskanal
Constructed for the Olympic Games of 1972: the first stadium in the world especially for canoe slalom, along the Ice Canal in Augsburg
Le premier stade de slalom pour canoë du monde, construit pour les jeux olympiques de 1972
Il primo stadio del mondo per gare di canottaggio sull'Eiskanal, costruito per i giochi olimpici del 1972
El primer estadio del mundo con slalom para piraguas, construido para los Juegos Olímpicos de 1972 en el canal de Augsburgo

Der Botanische Garten lädt ein zu erholsamen Spaziergängen inmitten einheimischer und exotischer Pflanzen
The Botanical Gardens attract visitors for a relaxing walk in the setting of both local and exotic plants
Le jardin botanique où il fait bon faire des promenades au milieu des plantes locales et exotiques
Il Giardino botanico invita a passeggiate riposanti fra piante locali ed esotiche
El Jardín Botánico invita a dar un paseo en medio de plantas locales y exóticas

Der Zoo im Siebentischwald, beliebtes Ausflugsziel für Tausende
The Zoo in "Siebentischwald" ('Seven Table Forest'), a popular place for animal lovers to visit
Le zoo dans la forêt «Siebentischwald», lieu d'excursions très apprécié par les amis des bêtes
Lo zoo nel bosco di "Siebentisch", meta di moltissimi visitatori
El Parque Zoológico en el bosque «Siebentisch», lugar apreciado y frecuentado por los amantes de los animales

Der Siebentischwald, ein beliebtes Naherholungsgebiet am Stadtrand für...
The "Siebentischwald" ('Seven Table Forest'), a popular recreation area on the outskirts of the town for...
La forêt «Siebentisch» (des sept tables), un havre de repos proche très apprécié aux bords de la ville...
Il bosco di "Siebentisch", vicinissimo alla città e perfetto per ...
El bosque de «Siebentisch», una zona de recreo en las cercanías de la ciudad...

... Sportler, Wanderer und Radfahrer
... athletes, hikers and cyclists
... pour les sportifs, les randonneurs et les cyclistes
... praticare dello sport, fare passeggiate ed andare in bicicletta
... para deportistas, excursionistas y amantes de la bicicleta

Entspannung und Gastlichkeit am stadtnahen Kuhsee
Relaxation and hospitality at the nearby "Kuhsee" ('Cow Lake')
Détente et accueil aux bords du lac «Kuh» (de la vache) proche de la ville
Una pausa di svago e di piacere al vicino laghetto di Kuh
Relax y hospitalidad gastronómica en el lago de «Kuhsee», cerca de la ciudad

Der Hochablaß, die Wasserversorgungsanlage mit Stauwehr am Lech, bereits im frühen Mittelalter angelegt
The "Hochablaß", the water supply plant with barrage on the Lech, constructed in the early Middle Ages
Le «Hochablaß», l'installation d'alimentation en eau et son barrage sur le Lech, construit déjà au moyen-âge
L'impianto di rifornimento d'acqua con diga sul fiume Lech, detto "Hochablaß", venne iniziato già nel Medioevo
El «Hochablaß», un sistema de abastecimiento de agua construido a principios de la Edad Media, con su embalse sobre el rio Lech

Augsburg im Frühling, der Residenzturm im Fronhof inmitten herrlicher Blütenpracht
Augsburg in bloom, the Feudal Court's Residence Tower amidst a magnificent luxuriance of flowers
Augsbourg fleurit, la tour de la Résidence dans la cour «Fronhof» au centre d'un splendide apparat de fleurs
Augusta in primavera, la torre della Residenza nel Fronhof circondata da un mare di fiori
Augsburgo en primavera, la torre residencial del «Fronhof», inundada de flores